D1143315

Editor: Heather Dickson

Authors: Nick Daws *(The Logical Burglar, Escape from Stone Island and Murder on the Menu)*, Christine Pountney *(Bad Business, Double Cross, The Perfect Heist, The Final Analysis and The Red Poppy)*, Richard Skinner *(Laundering Money, Wheels of Fortune, A Matching Pair and Two Up, Two Down)*

Additional contributors: Lorna O'Connell, Russell Walton, Rosie Atkins

Illustrator: Anni Jenkins

Page layout: Linley Clode

Cover design: Gary Inwood Studios

Published by: LAGOON BOOKS
PO BOX 311, KT2 5QW, UK

ISBN: 1899712283

Printed in France.

FIVE-MINUTE
CRIME LATERAL
THINKING
PUZZLES

OTHER TITLES

Five-Minute Lateral Thinking Puzzle Books

Five-Minute Murder Lateral Thinking Puzzles ISBN 189971233X
Five-Minute Classic Lateral Thinking Puzzles ISBN 1899712291
Five-Minute Adventure Lateral Thinking Puzzles ISBN 1899712348

Mind-Bending Puzzle Books

Mind-Bending Lateral Thinking Puzzles ISBN 1899712062
More Mind-Bending Lateral Thinking Puzzles - Volume II
ISBN 1899712194
Mind-Bending Lateral Thinking Puzzles by Des MacHale
ISBN 1899712232
Mind-Bending Conundrums and Puzzles ISBN 1899712038
Mind-Bending Classic Logic Puzzles ISBN 1899712186
Mind-Bending Challenging Logic Puzzles ISBN 1899712240
Mind-Bending Classic Word Puzzles ISBN 1899712054
Mind-Bending Crossword Puzzles ISBN 1899712399

**All books can be ordered from bookshops by quoting
the above ISBN numbers. Some titles may not be available in
all countries. All titles are available in the UK.**

INTRODUCTION

This book contains a collection of some of the world's best lateral thinking puzzles, hidden deep in the heart of 12 cunningly written crime stories.

Whether read alone or out loud for all the family to ponder over, they are guaranteed to provide hours of entertainment, mystification, contemplation and (ultimately) delight.

Each short story is about a different crime - be it about a burglary, a case of tax evasion, a murder or a suspected fraud - and takes around five minutes to read. How long it will take to answer the question posed at the end of each story, depends on whether you work it out for yourself, or resort to deciphering the mirror writing solution provided after each story.

(The answer to each puzzle is in mirror writing - this will stop an accidental glance spoiling the fun. Just hold the page up to a mirror for the answer to be revealed.)

INDEX

THE LOGICAL BURGLAR

THE LOGICAL BURGLAR

Rupert De Vere sat up suddenly in bed. He was sure he'd heard something. He waited a moment, then it came again: the unmistakable creak of a floorboard. He held his breath. He was certain he could hear footsteps down below.

Burglars, by heaven! Or at least, he corrected himself, a burglar; there was nothing to indicate that there was more than one. How had the blackguard managed to evade his state-of-the-art electronic security system, not to mention the Dobermanns? Well, there was one way to find out - catch the fellow and wring the truth out of him.

Rupert swung out of his king-sized bed. Though a big man, he moved with cat-like grace, a testament to the many hours he had spent in his own private gymnasium. He put on his robe, and picked up the heavy iron poker he kept by the bed. He had a feeling this precautionary measure was about to pay off handsomely.

Opening the bedroom door, Rupert listened once more. For a moment all was silent, then he heard a door opening (or closing, he corrected himself) downstairs. Quickly he moved to the banister rail and looked over. He saw a flash of torchlight, then the door to the music room closed with a barely perceptible click.

Rupert paused to take stock. The burglar - for it was clear now that there was only one - was in the music room. From there, the only place he could go was the study. He would have to come out the same way he had gone in, and Rupert De Vere would be waiting for him. Grim-faced, Rupert made his way downstairs, and positioned himself by the music room door with one hand on the light switch.

As he waited, listening to the noises within, Rupert wondered who this ingrate might be. Though born into a wealthy family, he had always done his best to help those less fortunate. He held no particular brief for the poor - most, he suspected, brought their woes upon themselves - but he had long ago promised his father he would look out for the underclasses. And, above all things, Rupert De Vere was a man who stood by his word.

Eventually the footsteps came nearer. The door opened and Rupert flicked the switch, bathing the hallway in light.

Before him, Rupert saw a spindly young man dressed in black. His expression was one of total bewilderment. Under his arm he held one of Rupert's most treasured possessions, an early painting by Picasso.

"Got you!" Rupert advanced menacingly, waving the poker in the burglar's face. The man dropped the painting and, as Rupert had anticipated, fled towards the study. Pausing only to check that the Picasso was undamaged, Rupert pursued him, bellowing loudly.

He followed the burglar into the study and put on the lights. The burglar cowered in front of the leather-topped writing desk. Rupert raised his poker as though to strike. The burglar's eyes bulged. He let out a small, almost child-like, scream. "Please, don't hurt me. I never did you any harm."

Still holding the poker high, Rupert took another step forward. Then he reached behind him and slammed the door shut. He turned the key in the lock and put it in his pocket.

"Right," he said matter-of-factly. "You're going nowhere, my lad. Not till you've told me how you got in."

"What..?" The man was still convulsed with terror. His eyes hadn't left the poker in Rupert's hand. Realising he would get no sense from the burglar in this state, Rupert put the poker down on the desk, keeping one hand close by. The burglar seemed to relax very slightly.

"Well, now," Rupert began, as though speaking to a backward child, "you evaded my security system, which the consultant assured me was impossible. So I need to know how you did it. I'm a reasonable man. Tell me how you broke in, and I will give you a choice about your fate."

The terror on the burglar's face began to fade, and was replaced by a calculating look. "You mean, if I tell you how I got in, you'll let me go?"

"You snivelling little..." Belatedly, Rupert remembered this man might have come from a deprived background. He could not be blamed for the lifestyle he had chosen - not entirely, anyway. "I didn't say that," he continued in milder tones. "I merely said I would give you a choice over your fate. And Rupert De Vere always keeps his word."

"All right then." The burglar looked resigned. "The first thing you should know is that any security system's weakest link is the person using it. I've been observing you for weeks now. You're a man of fixed habits, Mr De Vere. That's dangerous in itself."

Rupert stared at the burglar. "How come I've never seen you before?"

"I kept my distance, Mr De Vere, and I have a few tricks of my own. I have a pair of high-powered binoculars with infra-red vision. From a tree on the edge of your estate, I could watch you keying the numbers into your security system. I didn't get them all at once, of course, but eventually I had the entire sequence. So that's one lesson for you - change your numbers often."

"I see. Yes, good." Rupert scratched his chin. He could see that he

would need to make another appointment with the consultant.
"But the Dobermanns in the garden - how did you avoid them?"

"Like I said, Mr De Vere, you're a man of fixed habits. Every evening at seven o'clock you take them for a walk round your estate. So tonight, while you were round the back, I let myself in through the front gate and made my way into the house. I entered, using your security code and re-armed the system once I was in. Then I simply waited in a downstairs closet till you had gone to bed. Everything went like clockwork...till you found me, of course."

"Excellent!" Rupert boomed. "You really have been most co-operative."

"So what about your part of the bargain? You said you'd give me a choice."

"And so I will. I keep my promises...even with thieving little scumbags like you." Rupert picked up the poker again, watching with satisfaction as the burglar cringed.

"As you've helped me, I'll give you the opportunity to choose your fate. You must make a statement. If it is true, I will call the police. If it is false," Rupert laughed harshly, "I'll throw you to the dogs!" He laughed again. "So think carefully, lowlife, then speak!"

The burglar thought long and hard. De Vere's choice seemed no choice at all. Then a smile brightened his face. He realised, suddenly, there was a way out.

Faced with either being handed over to the police or being thrown to the dogs, what could the burglar say to avoid punishment?

SOLUTION

The burglar could say: "I will be thrown to the dogs.", for it would leave Mr De Vere, a man who says he always keeps his word, with no choice but to let him go.

If he did what the burglar said and threw him to the dogs, then the burglar's statement would have been true, so De Vere should have called the police. If he handed him over to the police, then the burglar's statement would have been false, and he should have thrown him to the dogs.

The burglar's logical response made it impossible for De Vere to keep his word - he had no alternative but to let the man go.

ESCAPE FROM STONE ISLAND

Escape From Stone Island

It was well after 'lights out', but neither Grant Steinberg nor his cellmate Billy Adams were asleep. Billy was tired all right, but something Grant said had reeled him back from the Land of Nod.

"I'm getting outta here, Billy."

At first Billy had thought he was joking. "Sure, Grant. You've got your own private helicopter on the roof right now, yeah?"

There was a moment's silence from the upper bunk. "I'm not kidding, Billy. I don't know exactly how I'm gonna do it yet, but I'm leaving."

Billy sat up; he was wide-awake now. "You've gotta be kidding. No one's ever escaped from Stone Island. The only way you'll get out of here is in a box," he sniggered. "And don't tell me you're thinking of playing dead and escaping in a hearse either. Mad Robbie Roberts tried that three years ago. All he got was a bad case of 'flu from lying on the morgue slab for an hour." He laughed heartily. It turned into a long chesty wheeze, and he had to bury his face in his grimy handkerchief.

When at last all was silent, Grant spoke again. "Sure, laugh, Billy. But you'll be laughing on the other side of that ugly face of yours when I'm a thousand miles away - living it up with wine, women and song - and you're still rotting in this cell."

There was no more conversation, but Grant's words went round and round in Billy's head. Everyone knew that there was no escape from Stone Island. But, though Grant had been there for only a few weeks, Billy had soon discovered that he was clever...very clever. He still didn't think escape from The Stone was possible...but if anyone could pull it off, Grant could.

Next day at breakfast, Billy and Grant shared a table with Scissors Smith and Black Sandy MacDonald. In earlier life Smith had been a ladies' hairdresser, though later he put his skills with a blade to different use. No one knew what Black Sandy had done, but even the guards called him Sir. This morning, however, he seemed unusually cheerful, only glaring and cursing good-naturedly at Scissors when he made the mistake of helping himself to the ketchup before Sandy had emptied it.

"You're in a good mood today, Sandy," Billy observed.

"And why shouldn't I be? I'm on garden duty again."

"Garden duty?" Scissors said through a mouthful of fried egg. "Nothing grows on Stone Island apart from a few weedy shrubs."

"Exactly," Sandy said. "And I'll be lying out in the sun watching them, making sure none of you heavy-footed bastards treads on one." He glared around the table, but no one dared say anything.

"What about you, Scissors?" Billy asked.

"Me? Oh, you know. Just another day in paradise. This morning I'm meeting my aromatherapist, then a light lunch at a beachside bistro with a lovely young lady of my acquaintance, followed by a drive round the island's beauty spots, and a cooling dip in the sea."

Billy sniggered. "Watch out for sharks then. You know how Hopalong Harry got his name." He nodded towards a thick-set, morose-looking individual eating alone in the corner. "Harry thought he'd swim back to the mainland, but he only got fifty yards before one of them bit his leg off. Rumour has it, by the time he'd scrambled back to Stone Island they'd bitten off another appendage as well."

Grant had sat silently through these exchanges, a faraway look in his eye. Now he leaned forward. "Could you drive around the island?" he asked.

Billy shrugged. "Maybe, if you had a four-wheeler. But there are no cars here."

"Catch a bus, maybe," Scissors said. "One every hour."

"You're a facetious bastard," Sandy snarled, leaning forward aggressively. "You're as likely to see a fairy as a bus on this island." He glared at Scissors. "*Much* more likely to see a fairy."

There was an awkward silence. "What are you doing today, Grant?" Billy asked.

"Thought I'd walk down to the guard house. Want to come,

Billy? Take a morning off the day job?" Billy worked in one of the prison workshops assembling small leather items: darts cases, wallets, and so on. The pittance he received paid for a few little luxuries like sweets and cigarettes.

"The guard house? I dunno why you want to go there." Billy shrugged. "Oh sure, what the hell."

A little later the two men were walking towards the island's guard house at the end of the bridge which was the only way in and out of the island. As usual, it was a warm day with only the softest of breezes. Billy couldn't remember the last time there had been anything you could rightly call a wind.

"You know last night?" Billy began, as soon as they had passed out of earshot of the others. "When you said you'd be leaving The Stone - you were joking, weren't you?"

Grant stared back at him. He continued to walk steadily up the incline. "I never joke, Billy. I thought you'd know that by now."

"Well, how are you going to do it? There's only one way in or out of this prison and that's the bridge. And the guard won't let anyone leave without the proper release papers."

Grant narrowed his lips but he didn't say anything. Once they were a few hundred yards from the main prison buildings, they turned and looked back. The prison was a squat, sprawling mass of stone. The buildings rose from the scrubland like huge, grey boils.

"Ugly, isn't it?" Billy said.

"Sure is." Grant put his hand to his brow to shade his eyes from the sun. He seemed to be looking at the horizon.

"I wonder why they built it so flat," Billy mused.

"Why not?" Grant said. "There's plenty of space, so they could spread out as much as they wanted. And with one-storey buildings, if you throw yourself off the roof, the most you're likely to do is break an ankle."

"You've got all the answers, haven't you?" Billy said.

"Not yet, Billy," Grant muttered. "But I soon will."

They walked on to the brow of the hill. As they reached it, the bridge to the mainland appeared below them. The bridge was made of steel and concrete and was hardly a thing of beauty - its most impressive feature was its length. The far end, where it joined the mainland, was almost invisible through the spray.

"How long would it take to walk, do you think?" Grant asked.

Billy shrugged. "Half-an-hour at normal pace, I reckon."

They continued a little further, 'till they could clearly see the guard house on the island side of the bridge. Grant stopped. "That's far enough," he said. A few hundred yards away, they could see the guard staring out across the bridge. Even at this distance, the outline of the sub-machine gun at his hip was unmistakable.

"His name's Stan," Billy said, more to break the silence than anything else. "He's on duty twenty-four hours a day."

"Sounds like he's even more a prisoner here than we are," Grant said. "What kind of man is he?"

Billy shrugged. "Tough, no sense of humour, totally dedicated." A bit like you, Billy thought of saying, but didn't. An idea occurred to him. "If you're thinking of trying to bribe Stan, forget it. He may not be too bright but he's totally incorruptible. The last man who tried it spent a fortnight in the hospital wing."

"How about visitors from the mainland?" Billy could see wheels turning in Grant's brain, though what answers they might be coming up with Billy couldn't imagine. "How does he treat them?"

"He's polite, businesslike, efficient - as long as they have the right papers, of course."

"What if they don't?"

"Then he sends them away." Billy shrugged. "That's how it is. No one gets in or out of The Stone without papers. So unless you have a printing press hidden somewhere in the cell, and a supply of the governor's headed paper..."

"I haven't."

"No." Billy bit his lip. "I didn't really think you did."

Grant said no more, and Billy saw that he was staring down at the guard house again, where the tiny figure of Stan was still staring resolutely across the bridge towards the mainland. "Doesn't he ever take a break?"

"Oh, sure. He is human, you know." Billy grinned. "At ten o'clock in the morning, after he's finished his paperwork, he goes for a five-minute tea break. He knows he can do that because the bridge is two miles long."

Grant's eyes narrowed. "How's that again?"

Billy preened himself. He was enjoying the unaccustomed experience of being the one with all the answers. "Well, the gate at the far end of the bridge is always open - unless Stan pushes the panic button, of course. So if you could run to the far end during the five minutes he's supping his Earl Grey, you'd be free."

"Five minutes," Grant said thoughtfully. "That doesn't sound impossible for a man who's in good condition."

"You think so?" Billy was warming to his subject now. "I checked in the prison library. The world two-mile record is seven minutes, fifty-eight seconds. If you think you can cut three minutes from that, be my guest." He waved a hand towards the guard house, where the tiny figure of the guard could be seen moving. "He's going for his break now. Stan's so predictable you could set your watch by him. You've got exactly five minutes, if you think you're up to it. But remember, getting half-way or even three-quarters of the way is no good. If he sees you escaping when he comes back from his break, all he has to do is push the button - the gates at the far end of the bridge will close and..."

Grant cut him off in mid-flow. "Maybe not today, Billy. But I will. In fact, tomorrow, at 10.37am, I'll walk through the gate at the far end of that bridge, and be out of this place forever."

Billy heard the news from Scissors Smith, and soon it was all round the prison. Grant Steinberg had escaped exactly as he had promised. Stan, unaware of the escape of one of the prisoners till he was summoned by an angry governor, had been in the guard house at the exact time Grant had walked through the open gates to freedom.

Grant had no release papers, or means of transportation, so how did he escape from Stone Island?

SOLUTION

Grant set off from the prison at 10.01am, a minute after Stan, the guard, had started his five-minute tea break. He walked quickly for three minutes then turned around to walk back towards the prison. When Stan returned to his watch at 10.05am, Grant was walking towards him. When he reached the guard house at 10.07am Stan thought he was a visitor. As he didn't have the necessary written permission from the governor to enter the prison, Stan sent him away - letting Grant walk through the prison gate to freedom thirty minutes later, at 10.37am.

A Matching Pair

A MATCHING PAIR

The fifth Duke of Snettersly patted his lips with a napkin and rang the small bell, neatly placed on the William IV mahogany dining table. When his butler, Grubler, came and cleared away his meal, the Duke stared out of the rain-streaked window and announced that he was retiring to bed for the night. The butler murmured an assent.

After his employer had gone to bed, Ronan Grubler walked up the steep staircase to his attic room. He took off his serving coat, hung it on a nail in the wall and sat down on the edge of his bed. He was a very worried man. Eddie wanted his £1,000 back and was coming to the duke's house at midnight to get it. If he didn't have the money by then, Eddie had said, he would personally see to it that Grubler never walked again. Grubler's palms sweated at the prospect of meeting Eddie's henchmen in an alley one dark night. Where was he going to get £1,000 by midnight?

On his night off the week before, Grubler had gone to a small club on the outskirts of the town where, he had been told, a game of poker was played regularly. He knocked on the back door of the building and was led down some steps into a dingy basement. Sitting round a green felt table were three men, already playing under a bright light. They looked up as Grubler walked in. Grubler could smell the cards and the money in big piles next to each man. He loved that smell.

He sat down in the seat that was indicated to him, took out his wad of notes and pulled in his chair. He didn't bet much on the first few hands, preferring instead to watch the others play. The man to his right, who had introduced himself as Eddie Grinhaus, was the man to beat. Grubler played for an hour and lost the money he had. He asked for some credit. Eddie narrowed his eyes at him and eventually nodded. From somewhere in the room, a man placed £1,000 in notes at his side.

After another hour of playing, Grubler was dealt two Queens, a Jack, an eight and a seven. He turned in the eight and the seven and got back another Queen and another Jack. Grubler couldn't believe his luck. He tried to stay calm. The betting went round and one of the men folded. Eddie Grinhaus upped the stake. Grubler saw him, but the other man folded too. Eddie upped the stake once more and Grubler not only saw him, but raised the stake with all the money he had left. Eddie called his bet and asked to see his cards. Grubler put down his three Queens and two Jacks. "Full House," he said. Eddie looked at him and laid four Aces on the table.

When Grubler saw those Aces, they were like red rags to a bull. He jumped up and threw the table over, shouting that Grinhaus was a cheat. Before he knew what was happening, two men had pinned him to the ground. Eddie leant over a few inches from his face and told him to have the money by next week.
Then, he was unceremoniously dragged up the steps and thrown out of the club.

Grubler shuddered at the memory. He stood up and walked over to the window, from where he could see the trees in the grounds of the estate shaking in the storm. Just then, Grubler heard the front door bell. He looked at his watch - 10.45pm. Eddie was early! He ran down the flight of stairs to the grand staircase overlooking the hallway. He jumped the last few steps to the door and opened it. Eddie stood in a fedora hat and trenchcoat, flanked by a man who was as wide as he was tall.

"Hello, Ronan." Eddie said. "May we come in?"

Eddie didn't wait for an answer but walked straight in. He left a puddle where he stood, looking around at the gold-painted balustrade and plush red walls. "Quite a place you live in, Ronan, shame you might be leaving so suddenly."

"Listen Mr Grinhaus, I don't have the money at the moment, but I can get it for you."

Eddie tutted. "Floyd here don't like not getting what he's due, do you Floyd?"

The big man shook his head and took his hands out of his Burberry raincoat.

"Where's the money, Ronan?" Eddie said, narrowing his eyes.

Grubler looked at him and knew he would be harmed if he didn't come up with an idea. "OK Eddie, wait here. I'll get it for you," he said and walked down a hallway towards the west wing of the house. He opened a door that led into the dining room and switched on the light. He paced the room not knowing what to do. A long rosewood sideboard which housed the cutlery and candlesticks stretched along one wall. He sat on it, thinking that he would have to come clean.

Then, suddenly, it dawned on him that he was sitting on the solution. The candlesticks! The Duke took a special pride in them. He would make a point of always telling Grubler what they were worth before he had to polish them. How could he ever forget that the Duke had three matching pairs of George III silver candlesticks and four matching pairs of Victorian parcel-gilt torchères? Individually, each candlestick was worth £250, but a pair was worth £1,000. The Duke had so many he would never notice - he could steal a pair and pay Eddie! Of course!

Grubler went to open the cupboard but, just as he did so, he heard a tremendous crack outside and then the lights went out. A tree must have fallen in the storm and brought down the wires. He heard Eddie shout his name. Panicking, Grubler reached inside the cupboard but realised that he couldn't tell the candlesticks apart in the dark.

How many candlesticks would Grubler need to steal in order to be sure of having a matching pair to give to Eddie to pay off his £1,000 debt?

SOLUTION

Three. As there were only two types - George III or Victorian - even if he grabbed one of either type, the third would have to match one or the other.

DOUBLE CROSS

DOUBLE CROSS

Jerry Wise had spent the last ten years of his life climbing up through the ranks to achieve the status of auctioneer at Sotheby's. He was thirty-two and an expert in antiques, especially from the period between 1914 and 1918. He had an extensive personal collection of memorabilia from the Great War, and had a particular passion for medals awarded for heroic action in battle. Jerry came from a poor background and feared, more than anything else, some kind of personal or financial crisis that would force him to return to his childhood ghetto.

One night, Jerry had a terrifying dream in which he lost his job, then his beautiful flat and his Saab Turbo 9000, and was reduced to living in the cardboard village under Waterloo Bridge. When he woke up, he was shaking. He went to the bathroom and splashed cold water on his face. As he was looking at his face in the mirror, Jerry vowed to devise some way to guarantee his own financial security. Jerry wanted to feel safe and he was prepared to risk everything in the process.

Jerry Wise locked the door to his office and sat down at his big mahogany desk. He pressed a knob under the second drawer and a secret compartment opened. He took out a hard, black leather case the size of a mouse trap and raised the lid. He stared at its contents, then snapped the case shut and put it in his briefcase. Jerry looked at his watch and checked it against the clock on the wall. He straightened his tie and made his way downstairs to the auction room.

Jerry took his place behind the podium, opened up the log book, signed his name and recorded the date. He looked out at the faces in the crowd and identified the four main players in the room. Mrs Witherspoon, a Sotheby's regular who had more money than sense, was sitting in the middle of the third row; to her left was an expert dealer by the name of Mr Wager; two rows further behind sat Miss Hardy, a representative of the fourth Earl of Dulverton; at the very back of the room stood a tall, thin, pale young man in a borrowed jacket and tie. The young man fidgeted nervously with his bidding paddle and shifted his weight back and forth from one foot to the other. Jerry handed the small, black leather case to his assistant and brought his gavel down hard on the block. The auction had begun.

Mrs Witherspoon attended auctions as religiously as some people attended church. She never missed an opportunity to come to Sotheby's and spend some of her husband's money. She wasn't particularly discerning and had been known, in the heat of the moment, to bid far more than an object was worth. Mrs Witherspoon cleared her throat and pulled at the hem of her pink Chanel suit that was too short and too tight for her more-than-middle-aged figure. She had read in the house catalogue that a very valuable military medal was up for auction and thought it might make a handsome gift for her husband's sixty-fifth birthday the following week.

Being an informed dealer, Mr Wager was also aware of the famous medal that was up for sale that day. He knew the real value of an object like that and was keen to purchase it. Some of his regular clients had strong connections with the military and would, he was sure, be interested in the medal. Mr Wager sat with his head bent over the Sotheby's catalogue, marking down the selling price of certain items in a little black book that he always carried in the breast pocket of his tweed blazer. He had a round and intelligent face, and was well respected by his colleagues. He was known to be a scrupulous businessman and never charged more for an item than he knew it was worth.

Mr Wager was a bachelor and lived in a cosy flat in Central London. He spent most evenings in front of his coal fire reading up on 19th and early 20th century collectibles, or brushing up on his knowledge of the two World Wars. He was scrupulous in all his dealings and never lied. Over the years, he had helped out many young dealers who came to him when they had difficulty placing or identifying an antique. Mr Wager's expertise was inexhaustible, and he could always be relied upon for an accurate estimate. People in the antique business said that it would be hard to find a more honest person.

Miss Hardy was also an honest person, particularly when it came to matters of the heart. She was not shy to admit the true nature of her business. She opened the catalogue on her lap and waited to bid for the items her employer had circled the day before. She had the Earl's best interests at heart and some people said that they shared more than just a passion for antiques. She sat primly in her seat and adjusted the horn-rimmed glasses on her pointed nose.

She was determined to buy the famous medal that the Earl had expressed such an interest in, and imagined the look on his face when she presented it to him. He might even be so delighted as to give her a kiss. Miss Hardy swooned in her seat and would have continued in this distracted fashion if it hadn't been for a gentleman beside her tapping her on the shoulder and enquiring as to whether or not she was feeling unwell. She gave a little cough and by way of a nervous reaction raised her blue bidding paddle and unwittingly became the owner of a harlequin set of six simulated bamboo side chairs, circa 1830.

The young man at the back of the room was also under the influence of some powerful emotion. He was noticeably affected by the proceedings. He kept wiping the sweat from his brow with a stained and crumpled handkerchief. He was a new face at Sotheby's, and his entrance caused some people to turn their heads. A wave of murmurs spread across the room as the young man shuffled towards the back and took his place behind the crowd.

The young man's name was Wolfgang Jaeger. He was the grandson of a notorious German war criminal who was killed by a young Welsh private, who was then awarded the Victoria Cross. Wolfgang did not know the private's name, but when he heard that a Victoria Cross, awarded to a Welsh private, was up for auction at Sotheby's, he was determined to buy it and bury it beside his grandfather's grave as an act of reconciliation.

The four main players in the room were eagerly awaiting the bidding on the last lot of the day, lot 307. After the sale was closed on lot 306, a silence descended on the crowd. A phone rang somewhere in another room of the building. Someone's wristwatch beeped four times, marking the hour. Jerry looked up at the skylight and swallowed. He could feel his heart beating rapidly in his chest. He picked up a glass of water from a little shelf below the podium, and took a sip. He licked his lips and looked out at the people gathered in the room.

Wolfgang coughed into his handkerchief, then held his paddle between his knees and wiped his sweaty palms on the legs of his trousers. He stood poised for the bidding. Mr Wager held up a pair of pince-nez glasses and brought the catalogue to his face to read the small print. He had a puzzled look on his face. Mrs Witherspoon patted her hair into place and put the catalogue to one side. She held her blue bidding paddle in both hands. Miss Hardy edged forward on her chair so that her whole weight was balanced precariously on the last inch of the wooden seat.

Jerry's assistant held up the black case and the crowd seemed to hold its breath in anticipation. He slowly lifted the lid of the velvet-lined box and revealed the shiny circle and bright red ribbon of the Victoria Cross. Jerry read out the catalogue description in a reverential voice.

"This," he said, "is the very prestigious Victoria Cross awarded for valour during the 1914-1918 war. On the face of the medal is the trademark bronze cross-pattée, the crown with a lion on it, and below that, the scroll on which are written the words For Valour during World War I. On the back, in the middle, is written 27 March 1916, the date on which the action took place. Engraved on the reverse of the suspender bar is the name of the soldier who was awarded the cross at the end of the war; Private J Jones, Welsh Regiment."

Wolfgang sucked in his breath and raised his numbered bidding paddle.

Jerry acknowledged his bid with a nod and started the bidding. "For lot 307, I've got an £11,000 bid on this. Now £12,000 with the gentleman at the back of the room. Do I have £14,000?"

Miss Hardy very excitedly waved her bidding paddle in the air.

"It's with you," Jerry said nodding towards Miss Hardy, "at £14,000. Do I have £15,000? £15,000?"

Mr Wager started to raise his paddle but stopped his arm in mid-air. He dropped the paddle back into his lap, lifted his hand and scratched his forehead. He looked from Jerry to the catalogue, then back at Jerry. He crossed his arms over his chest and raised one eyebrow. Jerry didn't notice Mr Wager's odd behaviour because he was too busy taking a bid from Mrs Witherspoon. She lifted her paddle and verbally raised the bid by £5,000, bringing the price up to £19,000. Wolfgang shook his head. This was going to be more costly than he had expected. He slowly raised his paddle and Jerry acknowledged the bid, and brought the price up to £20,000. Again, Miss Hardy gave an excited twitter and shook her paddle in the air.

"It's with you now, at £22,000," Jerry said and pointed to Miss Hardy. A voice off to the side of the room yelled out something and Jerry pointed to a woman seated at an elevated row of desks. "£23,000 on the phone", Jerry said. "I'm verifying that I have £23,000 on the phone? Yes? OK. It's with you on the phone. Do I have £24,000?"

"Thirty!" cried Mrs Witherspoon nearly jumping out of her seat.

"I've got £30,000 back in the room," Jerry said. "Do I have £31,000?"

Miss Hardy raised her paddle and Jerry took the bid up to £31,000. Wolfgang hung his head and raised his paddle again.

"£32,000," Jerry said and pivoted his outstretched arm to point to Wolfgang at the back of the room.

"£33,000," Jerry said, pointing at Miss Hardy.

"£34,000," he said, now pointing back at Wolfgang.

"£35,000," he said, pointing to Mrs Witherspoon.

Wolfgang raised his paddle again.

"£36,000!" Jerry shouted excitedly, eyes fixed on the thin young man at the back of the room.

"No!" Wolfgang screamed. "£46,000! I raise the bid to £46,000! Will anybody challenge me?"

Everyone in the room swivelled round to look at the young man. Wolfgang was even paler now. Little beads of sweat clung to his upper lip. People started to whisper among themselves again but Wolfgang stood his ground. He took in a deep breath and puffed out his chest. Then, in defiance of the mumbled insinuations, he held up his paddle as if he was saluting the crowd and repeated, "£46,000!"

Jerry began to smile. All the nervousness of the past few weeks started to fade away. He had to control the urge to chuckle to himself. He looked at Miss Hardy and raised his eyebrow as if to ask her if she was done. She pursed her lips together and briskly shook her head. Mrs Witherspoon tossed her bleached blonde hair to one side and threw her paddle on the floor. Jerry looked out at the hushed crowd. He raised his gavel and held it poised, ready to come down on the block.

"Are you done?" he asked the crowd. "It's with you," he said, pointing at Wolfgang. "I'm selling at £46,000 to the young gentleman at the back of the room. If there are no more bids, I'm closing at £46,000..."

"Stop!" somebody yelled. Jerry spun around to face Mr Wager. The shrewd old dealer had been puzzled throughout the whole proceedings. He'd been mulling over something that was nagging at the back of his mind and finally he had figured it out... just in time.

"Stop!" Mr Wager yelled again, jumping up from his seat and shaking his fist in the air.

"It's a fake!"

Mr Wager was right, but how did he know that the medal was a fake?

SOLUTION

The inscription on the back of the medal would not have read 'World War I' but rather 'The Great War', had it been a genuine medal, as no one referred to the 1914 - 1918 war as World War I until after the outbreak of World War II.

LAUNDERING
MONEY

LAUNDERING MONEY

Ray Statman watched the traffic move slowly down 6th Avenue from the back of the big yellow taxi. There was a gridlock all the way down to West 33rd Street. Ray was late for his meeting with the chief of police, so he got out and gave the taxi driver $20. The driver gave him the change and nodded. Ray walked towards the Penn Plaza building on the next block. In the elevator, he pressed the button for the eighth floor and checked his change - the taxi driver had short-changed him by $5. Damn, he thought, I hate it when that happens.

As it turned out, the chief of police was later than Ray, but no less angry for that. He berated the performance of the New York Police Department in failing to catch the city's biggest fraudster, Joe 'Pincer' Celeste, and appealed to the Board of Directors sitting at the other end of the table to do all they could to nail him.

After the chief had left, Ray picked up his briefcase and stood talking with other minor employees of Collins & Munroe City Auditors about the job in hand. They all agreed it was going to be difficult - 'Pincer' Celeste had successfully turned all his illegal gambling, soliciting and narcotics businesses into legitimate cover operations. Everyone knew he was crooked, but with Celeste's connections to the city's highest judges and best accountants, it had always been difficult to prove.

Ray walked to the elevator, thanking his lucky stars that it wasn't his responsibility to prove the impossible. He got in and pressed the button for the twentieth floor. Just as the elevator doors were closing, Wallace Munroe walked in and pressed the button for the thirty-eighth floor. They stood next to each other and the elevator floated upwards.

"Well Ray," Munroe said, "what do you think about the chief's request?"

Ray coughed and said, "I think it'll be difficult, sir. Celeste is a smooth operator."

"You're right, it will be hard, that's why we've decided to put some of our best people on the job, including you. With your background in corporate fraud, we think you have the necessary experience to help tackle this. What do you think?"

"I'll do my best, sir."

"That's the least you'll do, Ray. Your secretary has all the files on Celeste that the FBI could give us."

The doors of the elevator opened.

"Let me know as soon as you have something," Munroe said and Ray walked out.

Ray spent all day in his office looking over Celeste's company records, tax returns and insurance policies. He could see that they had probably been cooked, but there was no evidence he could use. At five o'clock, people started leaving to go home, but Ray fixed another coffee and looked over Celeste's books again.

He was looking through the tax returns when he noticed that a laundry company of Celeste's, called Winnin' Linen, had bought a small laundromat on the corner of Rivington and Pitt for $70,000. Almost immediately, it had been sold for $140,000. Interesting, thought Ray. He looked further into the returns and saw that the same laundromat had been re-bought two months later for $280,000 and re-sold for $350,000, again almost immediately. Ray checked the column marked Profit Tax Returns, but nowhere could he see that Celeste's company had paid tax on the profit from the sales. Gotcha, he thought.

Ray went up to the thirty-eighth floor. Luckily, Munroe was still in his office. Ray showed him the books and pointed to the discrepancy. Munroe seemed pleased.

"I'll ring the chief," he said, "you go down to the station on Lexington. I'm sure the chief will want to call Celeste in. Good work, Ray, there could be a promotion in the pipeline for you if this pans out."

"Thank you, sir," Ray said and left.

Ray's first glimpse of Celeste shocked him. The man was a walking promise of violence. His eyes seethed with intent; his body was hunched, ready to pounce. He sat down in the interview room and continued to chew on his toothpick. Ray sat beside two senior officers and the chief. This was his moment.

Ray began by giving Celeste the facts of the two sales and ended by accusing Celeste of profit tax evasion. When Ray had presented his case, Celeste smoothed down his dark brown suit and looked Ray in the eye.

"Is that all you brought me down here for?" he said.

"I think that's enough," said Ray.

"You ain't done your sums right, Mr Taxman."

"What do you mean?"

Celeste leaned on the table. "Look," he said, "I bought that laundromat for $70,000 and sold it for $140,000, right?"

Ray nodded.

"When I bought it again for $280,000, the $70,000 profit I made was wiped out and I was left $70,000 in debt. When I sold the laundromat for $350,000, I broke even. You can't pin no profit tax evasion on me 'cause I didn't make no profit. I have absolutely nothing to declare."

Celeste leaned back in his chair and looked at Ray and the chief. No one in the room spoke.

"Now, if you don't have me down here for anything else, I suggest you let me go before I sue the NYPD and Collins & Munroe."

The chief turned to Ray.

"Well, Mr Statman?"

Ray looked down at the books in front of him and held his head in his hands. The chief turned to the duty officer. "Let him go," he said.

When Celeste had gone, the chief turned to Ray.

"I'll personally make sure you never have a job in this city again, Mr Statman," he said and left.

Ray sat alone drowning in misery.

Who was in fact correct in their calculations?
Did Celeste make a profit or simply break even, as he claimed?

SOLUTION

Celeste made a profit.

Despite his smooth talking, his maths doesn't add up. He made a profit of $70,000 on the first transaction and $70,000 on the second. The two transactions are independent - the fact that there is a difference of $140,000 between $140,000 and the $280,000 figure is irrelevant.

(Interestingly, in 1931, when US authorities were desperate to jail the gangster Al Capone, all they could pin on him was tax evasion. He spent eight years in prison.)

THE PERFECT HEIST

THE PERFECT HEIST

Cookie Malone used to be the American heavyweight champion. He'd held the title for five years until he received a devastating blow by a boxer who was, at the time, a relative unknown. When it became obvious that Cookie was not going to get up, the referee raised his opponent's arm and declared him the winner. While Cookie lay unconscious, surrounded by a growing number of trainers and medics, his heavyweight belt was passed on to the new champion, a young man by the name of Reg Swinger.

Cookie spent three weeks in a coma. When he regained consciousness, the doctor told him that he had sustained extensive damage to the right side of his brain. As a result, he was partially paralysed down the left side of his body. Ever since the accident, whenever Cookie smiled, the left side of his mouth remained inert, and the effect was a crooked smirk. This was how he acquired the nickname 'Crooked' which, after a while, was shortened to 'Crook'.

Now that his boxing days were over, Cookie could no longer afford to lead the life he was accustomed to. He had to take out a loan to cover his annual membership at the golf club but, after three years of virtual bankruptcy, the bank refused to give him any more credit. Cookie's membership expired and he began to lose touch with old friends because he could no longer keep up with their decadent lifestyle. Cookie grew bitter and desperate; he had no other formal training and didn't know how to make ends meet.

One day, while Cookie was at the bar, drinking his usual bourbon on the rocks, a man walked in, came over and sat down next to him. Cookie had seen him a few times before, but didn't know his name or his business.

"Hi there, Crook," the man said. "How's it going?"

"How do you know my name?" Cookie asked.

"Aw, come on," he said. "I know a crook when I see one."

"Don't I wish," Cookie said.

"What do you mean?" he asked.

"I mean, if I was a crook, maybe I'd be better off than I am right now."

"Is that a fact?" said the man and lowered his voice. "I might just be able to help you out on that score. Call me Fagan."

And so his fate was sealed; overnight, Cookie went from being referred to as 'Crook' to actually being one.

At first, Cookie started small - a broken shop window and an empty cash register, a few roughed-up parking lot attendants - but gradually his skills increased. It was almost ten years since he'd lost the heavyweight title and Cookie now moved in completely different circles. His new friends were drifters and grifters and most of them had no idea that he used to be a champ. He showed no trace of his former athleticism. Cookie had become a fat man; he was so fat that people had started calling him Cookie again.

One day, Cookie got a call from his sister in New Jersey. She told him that her son had been accepted into Harvard to do a bachelor's degree in abstract mathematics; the only problem was that they couldn't afford the tuition. More than anything else in the world, Cookie loved his sister's kids, Denis and Sharon. He'd watched them grow up and treated them as if they were his own. Before hanging up, Cookie told his sister not to worry; he would get the money if it was the last thing he did.

Cookie spent the next few weeks hatching a plan. One evening, after four bourbons, it finally came to him. The perfect heist.

When Cookie had been a champion and everyone wanted a piece of him, he had toured a bank with a potential benefactor by the name of Darcy Suede. Mr Suede had wanted to invest in Cookie's career. He was an investment banker and the president of a large firm that had just moved into a new eighteen-storey building.

Cookie could remember the layout of Mr Suede's office on the top floor. On the wall behind his desk, behind a framed picture of the city, was a medium-sized safe containing large numbers of unmarked bills. Mr Suede had shown him the contents in an effort to persuade Cookie of what he called, his 'financial viability'. As long as Mr Suede was still in business, Cookie had a set-up.

As he was drawing up his plan, Cookie realised that he couldn't do this on his own. He needed two accomplices. He ran his fingers over the short stubble of his shaven head, then replaced the tweed cap that he always wore. It was late in the evening and he knew his sister would be in bed. He dialled her number and Denis answered the phone.

"Denis," he said. "It's me, Cookie. Can you meet me, tonight? And bring Sharon along too. I've got a proposition to make."

Two weeks later, dressed in black, wearing black gloves and black ski masks, Cookie, Denis and Sharon broke into the Suede

Management Building, and climbed the seventeen flights of stairs up to the Suede Investment Banking offices on the top floor. Darcy's office was exactly the way Cookie remembered. Behind the picture of the city was a safe plastered into the wall. While Denis and Sharon took their posts as look-outs, Cookie prised the safe forward with a crowbar. With one last powerful jolt, the safe popped free and dropped to the floor with a crash.

"Shhh," Sharon whispered. "I think someone's coming."

Cookie knelt down by the safe and brushed the plaster dust off a little metal plaque above the combination lock. The plaque read: Average weight of safe, 84 lbs. Cookie squatted in the correct weightlifting position and heaved the safe up with his good right arm. He then motioned to his niece and nephew to follow him down the hall. Just as they were about to set off, a burly security guard stepped into the corridor, aimed his flashlight at Cookie's face and said, "Not so fast, buster."

Cookie stopped dead in his tracks. He recognised that voice.

"Reg? Reg Swinger? It's not you, Reg, is it?" Cookie asked.

"How do you know my name?" the security guard asked.

"It's me, Cookie," he said, pulling the ski mask up over his face.

"Well, I'll be..." Reg said.

"What happened to you?"

"I accepted Mr Suede's offer for financing. You know, the same deal he was trying to offer you. Only my career didn't last so long. I was a bad investment. When my boxing career caved in, Mr Suede gave me this job as night watchman. He said it was an equitable arrangement. I didn't see it like that at first, but I've gotten used to it."

"I think we should be getting out of here," Denis said.

"Good idea," Cookie replied. "It sure was lucky for us to bump into you tonight, eh, Reg?"

"I'm sorry, Cookie, but I'm still going to have to call the police."

"What about for old times' sake?" Cookie pleaded.

"I'm just trying to do my job," Reg said, and walked forward with his arms extended, forcing the three thieves back into the office.

"What about the kids?" Cookie exclaimed.

"You never were very bright, were you?" Reg said. "Looks like you've lost again."

Cookie was speechless. He watched Reg raise his walkie-talkie to his mouth and report the intruders, then close the door and lock it. Denis and Sharon looked at each other.

"How long have we got before the police arrive?" Denis asked.

"It's eleven o'clock right now. They'll be here in fifteen minutes," Cookie said, and started to put the safe down. "I'm so sorry guys. I've really done it this time. How will your mother ever forgive me?"

Denis ran over to the window, looked outside and said: " Look, Cookie, there's a window cleaner's pulley hanging outside. There are two empty buckets at either end for taking the window cleaner up and down the outside of the building. We could use the safe as a counter-weight and escape in one of the buckets."

"It's not going to be that simple," Sharon said. "There are some instructions here. It says: DO NOT put any combination of people in the descending bucket if the total weight exceeds, by 25 lbs, the weight in the ascending bucket; otherwise, the bucket will descend too rapidly making it hazardous for human transportation. From a height of eighteen floors, approximate time of descent is one minute."

"What else does it say?" asked Denis.

"The descending bucket cannot weigh less than the ascending one," Sharon answered.

"OK," Denis said. "How much do you weigh, Cookie?"

"210 lbs."

"And you, Sharon?"

"I weigh 98 lbs," she said.

"And I weigh 120 lbs," said Denis. He paused as he did a series of quick calculations in his head. "We can do it!" he shouted. "We can do it!". He looked at his sister then across at Cookie and asked "How much time do we have left?"

Cookie looked at his watch. "It's three minutes past eleven. That means we only have enough time to make eleven trips in the pulley with one minute to spare."

Denis smiled. "Don't sweat it, Cookie. We're gonna get you out of here."

With only a window cleaner's pulley as a means of escape, and with only twelve minutes left before the police arrive, could Denis, Cookie and Sharon escape to freedom with the safe? And if so, how?

SOLUTION

Yes, they could escape with the safe in 11 journeys (see below), which would mean they would be free by 11.14pm, giving them one minute to spare.

Journey 1: Safe down, empty basket up. Journey 2: Sharon down, safe up. Journey 3: Safe left at top, Denis down, Sharon up. Journey 4: Sharon left at top, safe down, empty basket up. Journey 5: Cookie down and Denis and safe up. Journey 6: Denis out, safe down, empty basket up. Journey 7: Sharon down, safe up. Journey 8: Safe left at top, Denis down, Sharon up. Journey 9: Sharon left at top, safe down, empty basket up. Journey 10: Sharon down, safe up. Journey 11: Sharon gets out and safe should come down automatically.

WHEELS OF FORTUNE

WHEELS OF FORTUNE

Arabella, Miriam and Lucy sat on their balcony in the morning sunshine. In the harbour below them, the Sydney Opera House was like a stack of conch shells. Arabella sipped her tea. It would be freezing in London right now, she thought.

"When's Guy coming round?" Lucy said.

"Any minute now," Arabella replied.

Lucy looked worried. "Who is he again?" she said.

Arabella put her cup down. "I told you, Lucy, he's a friend of a friend of mine. He's a mechanic."

"I just don't want to hand over $3,000 to a total stranger, that's all."

"Look, we want to enjoy our year here, don't we?"

"Of course we do," Lucy said.

"Well, we don't know anything about vans, so we have to get an expert opinion. Don't worry, I'm sure he'll be fine," said Arabella and got up to answer the doorbell.

Guy strode confidently onto the balcony, followed by Arabella, and his face broke into an easy smile. "G'day girls," he said.

He sat down and listened as Arabella told him about their plans to travel around Australia. They needed a campervan for a three-month trip, which would incorporate Melbourne, Adelaide and Perth. They would sell the van in Perth and fly back to Sydney with the money.

"That's a flamin' big trip you've planned there," he said when

Arabella had finished.

"Well? Can we get something for $3,000 that'll get us there?" Lucy asked.

"You'll need a good van. The terrain from here to the west coast is pretty rough and the climate is very hot and dry."

The three girls looked at him.

"But I think you can get something for your money. In fact, I saw a van last week that would be perfect, and it was about $3,000, if I remember rightly."

"Great!" Arabella said.

"When can we have a look at it?" Lucy asked.

"Tell you what, I'll go and look it over myself - save you girls the trouble - and if it's roadworthy, I'll buy it for you. How does that sound?"

Arabella looked at Miriam and Lucy.

"What if it costs more?" Lucy asked.

"I won't do anything if it's more than $3,000," he said.

Arabella looked at them again. Miriam nodded. Lucy sat back and studied Guy for a moment before finally agreeing.

"Good, it's settled," Guy said.

When the three girls had given him $1,000 each, Guy got into his 1976 Firebird, which he'd reconditioned from scratch, and drove home. He parked his car outside his house and took a bus to the address given for the campervan. When he arrived, he could see the van under a tarpaulin at the back of the house. A man answered the doorbell and said he would be glad to show him the van. Guy inspected the engine, making sure the carburettor and fuel injection were fine. He checked the radiator and suspension. Lying underneath the van, he looked over the brake pads and the chassis frame. Inside, he checked the electrics and the starting mechanism. Everything was fine.

Guy asked how much the van was and, to his surprise, the man said $2,500. Too many vans and not enough buyers, he explained. Guy said he'd take it and gave the man the cash. The man gave him the necessary documents and Guy drove off.

He arrived at the girls' apartment half-an-hour later. The girls were still sitting on the balcony.

"That was quick," Lucy said.

"You've just bought yourself one hell of a campervan," Guy said.

"How much did it cost?" Miriam asked.

"That's the best bit, it was $2,500. Cheap, eh?"

Even Lucy was impressed. "But is it roadworthy?" she asked.

"Of course it is! I wouldn't have bought it otherwise."

Guy gave them the documents and took out the rest of the money. He gave each of the girls $100 and asked "OK girls?"

Arabella smiled. "Thanks so much, Guy," she said.

He looked at her. "It's my pleasure." He put a further $200 on the table. "And that's for you to share between you," he said.

"Wait a minute," Miriam said, "that's not right."

Everyone turned to her.

"We each gave you $1,000. You've just given us back $100 each. That means we've each paid $900 towards the van, which totals $2,700. You've given us another $200 which makes it $2,900. You still owe us $100."

Guy checked his pockets.

"You owe use another $100!" she yelled. "You're trying to rip us off!"

"No, I'm not. I haven't got another $100"

"You must have, you liar!" Miriam screamed.

"Please calm down, Miriam," Guy said.

"No I will not. Not until you tell me where the missing $100 is?"

Lucy turned to Arabella and said: "I never trusted him in the first place."

"Don't look at me," Arabella answered back, "it's not my fault if he's a crook!"

"I'm not a crook!" Guy said.

"I'm going to call the police," Lucy said and walked indoors.

Within five minutes, two police officers arrived at the flat. But after listening to both sides of the story, they told the girls that they were not going to bring any action against Guy, since he had acted properly through out the transaction.

If Guy had acted properly through out the transaction, what had happened to the $100 which Miriam claimed was missing?

SOLUTION

There was no missing $100.

Guy was telling the truth about there only being $200 change to divide up between the girls. Each girl had paid $1,000, of which $833.33 was spent on the campervan ($2,500 ÷ 3 = $833.33). This means each girl was owed $166.67. They were each given $100 back, which means they were each still owed $66.67 ($66.67 x 3 = $200). Miriam's maths was faulty - that's all.

THE FINAL ANALYSIS

THE FINAL ANALYSIS

It was Roy Lester's first night on the job. After three years with the police force in Boston, he'd secured a position as homicide detective in a small town called Peaksville, located in a river valley of the White Mountains of New Hampshire. Roy was the only detective in town and worked the graveyard shift from eight in the evening to six in the morning. During the day, there were two policemen on duty, Bob and Shep Littlefoot.

That evening, when Roy arrived at the small police station for his first shift, Bob handed him the keys to the only police cruiser in operation and mentioned that he'd forgotten to fill the tank with gas. He said there was only enough gas left for a two-mile journey, and that the gas station was now closed until nine o'clock the next morning. He then said that, since Wednesday night in Peaksville tended to be very quiet, he would probably have no cause to take it out. Shep Littlefoot laughed and said that every night tended to be quiet and that Roy might find Peaksville a lot less stimulating than what he was used to coming from Boston and all.

Bob then showed Roy how to use the coffee machine and pointed to a box in the fridge that contained two jam doughnuts.

"I guess that's everything," Shep said.

"See you in the morning," Bob said and they headed for the door.

Roy followed them out onto the sidewalk and watched as they both got into their own Chevy pick-up trucks and backed out of their parking spaces. As they drove off in opposite directions, Roy felt a large raindrop land on his forehead, then another. Within seconds, it had started to pour. Roy stood in the doorway and watched the rain come down. A flash of lightning split the sky and a thunderclap shook the building. Roy closed the door and headed back to the office.

At eleven-thirty, Roy was nodding off in his chair. By midnight, the storm had grown worse, and Roy was woken by the sound of a branch smacking against the aluminium siding. He got up and went over to the window. It was dark outside and he saw his own reflection in the rain-streaked window. He cupped his hands around his eyes and pressed his face to the glass. He could make out the dark street and the dark shapes of trees swaying in the wet wind. Just as Roy was about to step back, he saw a hunched figure running down the street. He was bent over and leaning into the wind. He was running in a zig-zag fashion, as if he was very drunk. The man ran up to the building and Roy heard the door open and the wind howl through the corridor.

Suddenly, the man came bursting into the office. He collapsed into a chair and Roy noticed he had a thin cut down the side of his face, like a knife wound.

"I've been robbed," the old man said between breaths.
"A terrible thing. He just came upon me from out of nowhere. I tried to stop him. I must have surprised him. He had a knife."

"Try to calm down," Roy said and went over and poured the man a cup of coffee. "Here, drink this," he said.

The man took the cup and held it with both hands. He had white hair and must have been in his seventies. His shoes were soaked through, and the bottom of his trousers were black with muddy rainwater. Roy walked over to a closet and took out the first aid kit and a dry blanket.

"Here," he said and gave the man the blanket. "Let me look at that cut."

"Never mind about that," the old man growled.
"It's a shallow wound. Besides, I'm doctor here. I can do that myself. I want you to do your job. I want you to catch the culprit."

"Can you give me a description?" Roy asked.

"It must have been someone local. Someone who knows when I work late. I was in my office, you see. Everybody in town knows I have a safe there. I have nothing to hide. Many of my customers pay me in cash. They watch me open the safe. It's common knowledge."

"All right, sir, but can you give me a physical description of your assailant?"

"He was large," the old man said. "Over six feet tall and heavily built."

"Can you make a stab at his age?"

"This is no time for puns, young man!" the man barked.

"Forgive me. There was no pun intended."

"He was twenty-five, maybe. Between twenty-five and thirty," the old man said.

"Anything else?"

"I was being attacked!" yelled the old man.

"I realise that, sir," Roy said gently. "Any information that you can remember could help us."

"He had short, cropped, black hair. I remember that."

"Were there any other witnesses?"

"Not that I know of," he said, "although the lights across the street were on, at the offices of the Peaksville Gazette. Sometimes old man Harper works late, getting a last-minute story in. I know him well. He's a good journalist. The old-fashioned kind. Knows everything there is to know about this town."

"I'll keep that in mind," Roy said and walked over to his desk. He pulled out an assault report form. He picked up a pen and said, "Could I have your name, please?"

Before the old man had a chance to answer, the phone rang. Roy picked it up. "Hello?"

"Hello," came a faint, scratchy voice. "You don't know me, but my name is Mr Harper. I work for the Peaksville Gazette. I saw the whole thing happen."

"You were a witness?" Roy asked.

"Yes, yes. I saw everything. I know who it was. His name is..." The line went fuzzy and the voice was drowned out for a minute.

"Wait! Wait!" Roy yelled into the receiver and the voice came into focus again.

"He's the most dangerous criminal in the county," Mr Harper continued, and again his voice was scrambled.

"I'm coming over," Roy pronounced deliberately down the phone.

"You mustn't!" Mr Harper said. "I'm afraid. I've gone into

hiding." There was another flash of lightning, then a deafening rumble of thunder.

"We can protect you!" Roy yelled. "Mr Harper? Mr Harper? Can you hear me?"

Roy looked at the old doctor huddled in a blanket. "The line's gone dead," he said.

"What are you going to do?" the old man asked.

"All I have to go on is that he's the most dangerous criminal in the county. If he's on the loose, it's my duty to go and bring him in. I must arrest him without delay."

Roy crossed the room to the filing cabinet and opened the drawer marked 'Dangerous Felons'. He quickly sifted four suspects from the pile who fitted the description given by the old man. Roy placed the four files face-up on his desk and took out his notepad.

"Paperwork, paperwork, paperwork," the old man said. "Is that all you guys are good for these days? You've got four suspects. Why don't you go out and arrest them?"

"I'm afraid I can't do that, sir" Roy said. "There is only one vehicle at my disposal, with only enough gas in it for a two-mile journey. According to these files, each of the suspects is domiciled within a one-mile radius of the police station. However, every suspect lives more than a mile apart. I've only got one chance to get it right if I am going to go out and arrest the criminal and bring him back."

"What about back-up?" the old man asked.

"The phone lines are dead. Besides, the walkie-talkie in the car is hooked up to the radio in this office so that's no good to us either. No, this is a theoretical case. I've got to solve it in here first," Roy said tapping his temple with a finger.

Roy wrote the four names of the suspects across the top of the first blank page of his notepad. He drew three straight lines down to the bottom, setting each name apart in a column of its own. The names were: Fred Munch, Rex Hood, Bully Black, and Midge Fingers. Roy then bent over the files and studied them, taking notes whenever he came across a crucial piece of information. When he had finished, he sat back in his chair with a thoughtful look on his face. He ripped that page out of his notebook and wrote Final Analysis across the top of a fresh page. This is what he concluded:

1. Hood has committed more crimes than Munch and Black together. 2. Hood and Munch together have committed the same amount of crimes as Black and Fingers. 3. Fingers and Munch have committed far more crimes than Black and Hood together.

After a minute of careful deliberation, Roy jumped out of his seat and rushed over to the coat rack and grabbed his trenchcoat. He put his hand on the old man's shoulder and said, "I've got the culprit. Sir, you will be able to sleep peacefully tonight, knowing your assailant is securely behind bars."

"Thank you, young man. Thank you so much. But how do you know who to arrest?"

If the old man's attacker was the most dangerous of the four men, who did Roy plan to arrest?

SOLUTION

Fingers is the most dangerous of the four men.

You know that Hood is more dangerous than Munch and he is also more dangerous than Black. If Hood and Munch together are equally as dangerous as Black and Fingers, while Fingers and Munch are more dangerous than Black and Hood, then Fingers must be the most dangerous man, followed by Hood. Similarly, Munch is more dangerous than Black.

BAD BUSINESS

BAD BUSINESS

Miriam Timor looked up from her desk and watched her boss, Sheila Fanning, arrive at the office - twenty minutes late as usual. Sheila was an attractive woman, three years older than Miriam, who was always impeccably dressed in the most flattering business outfits and had her hair styled twice a week. Miriam knew this because she was the one who booked the appointments.

"You're in early again, Miriam," Sheila said. "Get me a cup of coffee, will you?"

As Miriam stirred the coffee, she wondered if now was a good time to tell her boss about the clause that had been overlooked in the paperwork for an important deal they were scheduled to make that week in Hamburg. Sheila had found a bank in Germany willing to back her investment in a new chain of hotels. It was a risky venture, however, if things went as planned, she expected to break even in the first year and begin yielding gross profits in the third and fourth. Miriam had found a paragraph in the small print that determined an inordinate interest rate on the loan. The paragraph also stipulated that the bank was not required to make this interest rate known to the client as it did not take effect until thirty-one days after the signing of the contract. Miriam was sure that Sheila would call off the deal if she was aware of these new figures. She hoped this find would earn her some recognition, maybe even a well-deserved pay rise, maybe even a promotion.

As she took the coffee in, Sheila asked: "Did you pick up my dry cleaning?"

"Yes," Miriam said. "It's in the foyer."

"Do I have any appointments this morning?"

"No."

"Then what are you waiting for?" Sheila snapped impatiently.

"It's just that I have something to tell you," Miriam said. "I don't know how to say this, but there's a flaw in the deal we're supposed to make this week."

"We?" Sheila repeated slowly.

"Well, you," Miriam said.

"What's wrong with it?"

"I'll go and get the paperwork," Miriam said and hurried out of the room. She returned with a copy of the contract and showed Sheila the paragraph in question.

"You know I don't know how to read German," Sheila said.

"It says that after thirty-one days, a fixed interest rate of fifty-seven per cent will be applied to the loan."

"Fifty-seven per cent!" yelled Sheila. "Are they out of their minds?"

"I thought you'd want to know," Miriam said softly.

"Well, of course I want to know. I want to know everything. It's your job to tell me everything. This was going to be the biggest deal of my career. What am I going to do? Leave me alone, Miriam. I have to think."

"Of course," Miriam said and started to gather up the paperwork.

"Leave that here," Sheila barked. "Now get out. I need to think."

Miriam shut the door behind her slowly and deliberately. She went over to her desk and sat down. After a while, the little red light on the telephone went on. She could hear Sheila's voice on the other side of the wall. She spent all morning on the phone. Eventually she emerged to call Miriam into her office.

"I want you to book two business class tickets. We're going to Hamburg."

"Still?" Miriam asked.

"Nobody messes with Sheila Fanning and gets away with it."

Two days later, at nine-thirty in the morning, Miriam and Sheila boarded a plane at Heathrow airport. They arrived in Hamburg at thirteen minutes past twelve. They took the airport shuttle to the city centre and checked into the Intercontinental. Miriam was given the key to a single room on the eighth floor, while Sheila was escorted by a bellhop to a lavish suite on the eleventh. At two o'clock, Sheila came down and knocked on Miriam's door to tell her she was leaving for the meeting "Let me just get my coat," Miriam said.

"Don't bother," Sheila answered. "I want to do this on my own."

"Are you sure?" Miriam asked.

"Positive."

"Well, in that case, I might as well do some sightseeing."

At a quarter to three, Miriam and Sheila stepped into separate taxis and headed out into the city.

Miriam returned to the hotel three and a half hours later. When she went to the front desk to pick up her key, the manager handed her three urgent telephone messages that were waiting in her mailbox. They were all from the bank; Sheila hadn't turned up for the meeting.

Miriam asked the manager to let her know as soon as Sheila returned, then went up to her room. After showering and changing, she ordered dinner. While waiting for her food, she sat on her bed and pulled the document on the Union Bank deal out of her briefcase. After flicking through it briefly, she slung it, along with an old ripped tissue, her boss' travel documents and a broken biro that she'd also found in the briefcase, into the hotel room bin.

At six-thirty, there was a knock on the door. "Come in," Miriam called, expecting her dinner on a tray, but instead of room service, a policeman walked in.

"Miss Timor," the policeman said as gently as possible. "I have some very bad news."

"What is it?"

"Sheila Fanning is dead," he said. "Her body was found in a skip behind the Union Bank."

"That's where she was heading this afternoon. This is terrible," Miriam said, and she started to cry.

"We are investigating the matter right now. We believe the approximate time of death to be between three and six o'clock. Could you possibly tell me where you were at this time?"

"I took a cab," Miriam sobbed. "We left together. You can ask the porter. He ordered the taxis. I went sightseeing and Sheila had a meeting with the bank. There were three messages when I got back. They said she never showed up."

"Thank you, Miss Timor," said the policeman. "Your testimony corroborates the manager's version of events. I am sorry about your friend. You are free to go. You are no longer a suspect."

When the policeman returned to the station, he filled out a report and met up with the homicide detective assigned to the case. His report showed that Miss Timor would not be held for further questioning. The detective was sceptical, but agreed that she was free to return to England. However, as a precaution, he rang up an old friend who worked for Scotland Yard and asked him to run a check on the young lady.

When Miriam arrived back at Heathrow the following day, the police were waiting for her - ready to arrest her.

The police arrested Miriam and charged her with the murder of Sheila Fanning - but what evidence did they have to pin the murder on her?

SOLUTION

The detective was sceptical about Miss Timor because he had found her boss' travel documents in her hotel room bin and, after checking with Scotland Yard, he had found out that she had booked the tickets for the trip - a return for herself and a one-way ticket for her boss.

Furious at having recieved no thanks for spotting the flaw in the German deal, and fed up with her boss's ungrateful treatment, Miriam had decided - while still in London - to kill Sheila Fanning in Hamburg - hence the purchase of only one return ticket.

When her boss told her she was going to the meeting at the bank alone, Miriam announced she was going sightseeing. But Miriam never laid eyes on any of Hamburg's tourist spots, instead she followed her boss to the bank and attacked and killed her when she got out of her taxi at the back door of the Union Bank. As Miriam did not return to the hotel until 6.15pm, she had plenty of time to hide Sheila Fanning's body in a skip.

Two Up,
Two Down

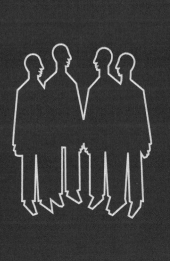

Two Up, Two Down

Two fathers and two sons lived together in a large, rambling house overlooking Marble Hill Park in Twickenham, South London. On the other side of the park, the River Thames flowed quietly into the city. They had moved there from Kilburn, years ago, and felt at home in the area. They knew many people and were well-liked.

The younger of the two fathers worked at Kew Gardens. He was a world expert in growing roses. When he was hired by the Trust in charge of the Gardens, he was given space in a special lab, annexed onto the back of the Palm House. He spent his working hours there carefully grafting various kinds of rose together and culturing the weird and wonderful hybrids in specially controlled environments. His results won many awards and drew large crowds of horticulturists to Kew.

When the Great Storm of 1987 struck southern and eastern parts of England, one of the tallest Scots Pines in the Gardens was uprooted and fell onto the lab. The morning after, the Trustees inspected the damage and grew morose. They sent the staff home and calculated the cost of repairs. Two days later, the Trustees called the younger father in and told him they couldn't afford to re-open his lab.

The younger father was distraught and went home to tell the others the terrible news. As the others were unemployed and had relied on his earnings to pay the rent, they all slowly

74

realised that they would have to move. The elder of the sons scanned the listings papers and viewed many houses, finally settling on a house in Camberwell which was big enough for them all and much cheaper than their house in Twickenham.

They moved into the house in Camberwell in January 1988. As they were still unemployed, they all applied for income support and housing benefit. Their housing benefit claims took a few weeks to process, but they were eventually each awarded £50 a month to cover the £200 rent. They all tried to find work, but were unsuccessful. During the following few years, the recession got worse and jobs became rarer. The younger father looked for work in all the gardens and small parks in the area, but was told that these were tended by council workers. In any case, if he were to apply to the council for such a job, he would be deemed overqualified.

Money was tight. Things got desperate. The younger of the sons, who had never had a job in his life, became depressed. His father tried to cheer him up, but was unable to, as he was too concerned about himself.

During the winter of 1990 - 1991, the other father became very ill. He was unable to get up and the others were worried about him. They called the doctor, who looked him over and diagnosed a bad case of pneumonia. The doctor didn't like prescribing antibiotics, but made an exception in this case.

Then one night, the younger of the fathers got a call from

the police. His son was at Camberwell police station, and would he come and pick him up. When he arrived at the station, the desk sergeant told him that his son had been arrested for shoplifting. He had stolen some cheese and some tins of beans and had been challenged by the store detective. After taking his details, the supermarket was prepared, in this case, not to press charges but warned, that if it ever happened again, they would prosecute. The father nodded and his son was handed over to him. They walked home and, after a while, the son apologised. The father patted him on the back and told him that it was OK.

On a bright morning in January 1991, the older of the fathers, now much better, was sitting down with his son, talking. They had just realised that it was exactly three years ago to the day that they had moved to Camberwell. Those three years had been the worst of their lives. They calculated that they had so far received £7,200 in housing benefit and hadn't done a single day's work.

Just then, the doorbell rang. The older of the fathers opened the door and saw three men standing there. Two were policemen, the other was a housing benefit officer. The older of the fathers demanded to know what they wanted. The housing benefit officer told him that he was investigating a case of fraud. His office had received a tip-off from an anonymous caller to say that they were claiming too much housing benefit.

The older of the fathers argued that each person in the

house was claiming £50 a month, which was what he was entitled to. The housing benefit officer agreed that, if none of them was in full-time employment, each man was indeed entitled to £50 a month in housing benefit. But, because they had received a total of £7,200 over the last three years, he was obliged to inform them that they had broken the law.

There was a long argument, during which both fathers became angry. The housing benefit officer realised that the situation could become violent. The policemen told everyone, including the two sons, to calm down, and informed them that they would have to come to the station. The younger father and elder son protested, but eventually, they were all taken to the police station and charged with fraud.

The housing benefit officer agreed that each man was entitled to £50 a month, yet he instructed the police to charge them with fraud all the same. Why?

SOLUTION

There were only three men - a grandfather (the elder father), a father (the younger father and elder son) and a son (the younger son) - not four, therefore they should only have collected £5,400 in benefits during the three years, not £7,200. They had indeed been defrauding the system.

THE RED POPPY

THE RED POPPY

Ronny Cage had been Chief Inspector of the Boston Metropolitan Police Force for seven years, and he was about to make the biggest bust of his career. One of his informers had tipped him off about a huge shipment of heroin coming into Boston on the 'Princess Moravia'. The ship was due to arrive in half-an-hour and Cage and his men were ready for her.

It was three-thirty in the morning and a dense fog had descended on the port. It was bitterly cold. Cage was wearing a thick overcoat with the collar turned up. He lit another cigarette from the burning tip of the one that he'd just smoked and flicked the butt into the black water. He walked to the edge of the dock and stared out into the mist.

Slowly and mysteriously, like some phantom vessel, the 'Princess Moravia' emerged from the fog. At first, all Cage could see were the two masthead lights; then the red and green lights on the ship's bridge appeared; finally, he could make out the yellow lights in the wheelhouse and the dark silhouettes of men at the helm. Cage watched as the huge ship slowly turned in the churning water and drifted towards the dock. The wall of the ship towered a hundred feet above him. The thick mooring lines were dropped and flung around the iron bollards. When the gangway was lowered, Cage gave the signal and his men boarded the ship to arrest the captain and ensure that no crew could escape. Six policemen were assigned to patrol the deck to make sure nobody jumped overboard.

By noon that day, a crane had lifted a hundred crates, containing more than two million dollars worth of pure heroin, out of the ship's hold. Cage had taken a crowbar to one of the crates when he first boarded the ship almost eight hours earlier. He had prised a few boards loose and reached his hand into the box. The boxes were marked: Finest Indian Tea, and sure enough, the first thing Cage felt were tea leaves, dry and brittle against his fingers. However, further down, Cage felt a hard lump wrapped in plastic, and withdrew the first pound of heroin.

All the crew members had been interviewed and released, but the captain was taken to headquarters for further questioning. He insisted that he knew nothing of the contents of the crates. He begged the police to believe that he was not responsible for the loading of cargo, but only for steering the ship.

"The crates were supposed to contain tea," the captain pleaded.

"I thought you said you knew nothing of the contents," Cage answered back.

"I don't," he said. "I read the label just like you."

After three hours of intense interrogation, Cage proposed to make a deal with the captain. He would let him return to his ship and give him clearance to sail out of Boston immediately, in exchange for the name of the person responsible for the shipment.

"I do not know his name," the captain said, "or else I would gladly give it to you."

"I need a name," Cage said.

"All I know is one thing," said the captain leaning forward conspiratorially. "I know that the man who is responsible for the shipment has recently been to Thailand and Hong Kong."

"What am I supposed to do with that information?" Cage yelled, getting up from his chair. "Book him!"

Cage went upstairs to his office and closed the door. He lit a cigarette and picked up the phone. "Give me Interpol," he said.

The following morning, Cage called four of his best men - John, Peter, Chris and Dan - into the operations room. He had cleared the table and laid out four separate stacks of files.

"Here are our four key suspects, gentlemen. Interpol has kindly provided us with all the information it has on the four most notorious drug smugglers working out of Asia. It has included extensive records of their whereabouts over the last six months including any movement across borders, especially Thailand and Hong Kong. What we have to go on is that the man we are looking for apparently made recent visits to both these places. My source at Interpol says, that in the last six months, each of these four men have visited two of the following places: Thailand, Nepal, Singapore and Hong Kong.

My guess is that, from these records, we should be able to pinpoint which one of them went to Thailand and Hong Kong. We should be able to make an arrest based on that information. It's going to be tedious work for you boys, but a job worthwhile if we get the right man. Now get to work. From now on, make it your top priority."

The first file was on Lin Su-Yung, a native of Hong Kong, who had completed his education at a boarding school in Britain, and now lived in a swanky apartment in Chelsea. He was said to be strictly a businessman, having never dabbled in drugs himself; but being tempted by the financial possibilities, had entered into the drug smuggling business as an entrepreneur. He had a tight network of very loyal henchmen, and tended to delegate jobs instead of getting directly involved. Occasionally, he made trips to Hong Kong under the pretence of visiting his family. Once he had set up the original connections, all subsequent deals were made through his various representatives. In all other respects, he was clean. He had no criminal record to date, and had not been to Thailand in the last six months.

The second file was on Brent Halloway. Brent had played college football for the University of California, where he was first arrested for possession of cocaine. When he didn't make it into the professional football league, he was forced to take a job in his father's construction company. He did not last long there - after only three months, he was arrested for possession again and, when his father bailed him out, it was on condition that he left the country. Halloway went to Thailand and after five years, was arrested on the border with Burma, on suspicion of opium and heroin trafficking. The charge was dropped because of lack of evidence.

Halloway returned to the States where he was believed to have set up an extensive drug smuggling ring. Although he had often been charged, he managed successfully to elude sentencing on every count. The authorities suspected he had contacts in the judicial system.

The third file was on Simon Fang, a one-time ballet dancer for the New York Metropolitan Ballet Company. It was on an international tour of 'Swan Lake' that he first acquired a taste for the 'Red Poppy'. The ballet company had done a performance in Singapore and Fang fell in love with the second violinist of the Singapore Symphony Orchestra. To the dismay of his company director, Fang stayed behind to marry the violinist. Two years later, they moved to Miami and set up a business importing textiles. The business now served as a front for drug trafficking.

Fang had good connections with drug manufacturers in Singapore through his wife's older brother, whom he had recently gone to visit. He was said to deal strictly in large amounts of heroin.

The fourth and last file was on Henry Willard, an ex-cop. Willard had attended the New York Police Academy and joined the force when he was twenty-three years old. When he was twenty-seven, he did a brief stint with the Boston Metropolitan Police Force, then transferred out to Los Angeles. Rumour had it that he found the level of corruption so disillusioning that he turned in his badge. Ironically, he surfaced six years later as a suspect in connection with a drug raid in San Francisco.

He was given a nominal sentence and released four weeks later on probation. Willard skipped probation and was later spotted in Hong Kong at a party given by Lin Su-Yung.

When Cage's men had gone through all the files, they sat around the table drinking coffee and discussing the case. Peter said, "So, as far as we know, there is no country which all four have visited. Is that right?"

"That's right, Sherlock," said his buddy, John.

"But each of the four men have, at one time in the last six months, visited two out of the four places: Thailand, Nepal, Singapore and Hong Kong," Peter continued.

"What I want to know," Chris interrupted, "is how does Interpol get this kind of information? I mean, these guys are elusive criminals, and yet Interpol has details on every day of their lives for the last six months."

"You're right," Dan said. "We've got all the clues right here in front of us. The answer is in this room. Let's get down to work."

"Good," said Peter. "According to my notes, it looks as if no more than one person has visited Singapore."

"I agree," John said. "This is what I've got. Only one country has been visited by three men and there is no common country which Su-Yung, Halloway and Willard have all visited."

"Good," Dan said.

"What about you, Chris?" Peter asked. "What have you worked out?"

"Well, looks like no one has been to both Nepal and Singapore."

"That's what my records show, too," Dan said.

"What's more," Chris continued, "it looks like Su-Yung has been to a country which Halloway has visited and also one that Fang has visited."

"Right," Peter said and started chewing his lip. "Do we have any other information that might be relevant before we chart this information out on the blackboard?"

"That's all I've got," Chris said.

"Me, too," John agreed.

"What about you, Dan?"

"Give me a second, Peter. I think I've got something here. Let me just verify this. We've already ascertained that Fang has been to Singapore, is that right?"

"Yes," Peter replied.

"OK," Dan went on. "Looks like Fang has been to Singapore, plus a country which Willard has also visited."

"Is that everything?" Peter asked. "All right then, let's chart out this information. I want a diagram on the board. Let's get this guy. Let's bring him home."

At four-thirty the following afternoon, Cage made a call to Interpol to notify it that he had identified the suspect and was making arrangements for his arrest and subsequent delivery to Boston to face charges of drug smuggling.

Who did Cage arrest and how did he know he was guilty?

SOLUTION

We know Su-Yung didn't go to Thailand or Singapore (only one person visited Singapore - Simon Fang) so he must have visited Nepal and Hong Kong.

Fang went to Singapore so therefore could not also have gone to Nepal. We know he visited a country Su-Yung went to - so this must be Hong Kong.

Willard went to a country Fang visited, and since we know only one person went to Singapore, this country must be Hong Kong.

Halloway went to a country which Su-Yung had visited. He therefore must have gone to Nepal (He couldn't go to Hong Kong because we know no country was visited by all four men.). The other country he visited must have been Thailand.

This means that Willard could not have visited Nepal (only one country was visited by three men - Hong Kong), so the country he visited, as well as Hong Kong, must have been Thailand. Willard was therefore the man to arrest.

MURDER ON THE MENU

MURDER ON THE MENU

Lieutenant Jake Strogani stifled a yawn. He stared at the station clock, which told him it was 2am. His shift had officially ended two hours ago, but Jake wasn't going anywhere till he had cracked this case.

Call it cop's intuition, call it what you will, but Jake knew that somehow Raph Minton was behind these four deaths. He stretched his arms above his head, took a deep breath, then began poring over his notes once more. Somewhere in those notes, there just had to be the clue he needed to put Minton back behind bars.

Prior to that fateful emergency call, it had been a quiet shift for Jake: a couple of drunk-and-disorderlies; a domestic in Lowtown which young Sally Barton had sorted out; a child with a lost dog; and the usual slew of traffic violations - hardly the stuff of police dramas.

Then the call came in. There had been an incident at a drinks party in Park Vale. Four deaths, possibly homicides. Sergeant Walters had taken the call. Jake overheard him recording the details: "So that's Ralph Minton? Oh, R-A-L-P-H, Raph. The Green House, Park Vale. Yes, I have that."

The name rang bells in Jake's head, and after a moment he remembered why. It was one of the earliest cases he had worked on. Thirty years ago, Raph Minton had been tried for the murder of his wife, Clara, and her lover. Minton appeared to have a watertight alibi. Somehow, however, the state prosecutors had broken it. Minton had gone down for second degree murder - lucky in the end to get away with that.

Minton always maintained his innocence, but in jail he was a model prisoner and got maximum remission. After fifteen years, he was released. He had stayed in the area, and Jake had followed reports of his progress with mild interest. A couple of years after his release, the local paper ran a story on how Raph had been named salesman of the year by insurance company Eternal Life. A few years later he set up his own financial planning company, Minton Associates; and now, ten years on, he was a multi-millionaire and a pillar of the local community.

And now this - four deaths - all senior partners in the law firm Smith, Knight & Winter. There was something familiar about those names, too. Jake decided to go along with his officers, Hall and O'Grady, to see what had happened for himself.

As they drove between the gates of Minton's luxury home, they passed an ambulance which was preparing to leave. The paramedic glanced out at them and shook his head. Hall parked in the drive, and the three made their way down the path towards the house. Distraught guests were spilling into the gardens. They passed a young man comforting a blonde woman who was in tears. Another young woman, with shoulder-length auburn hair, looked on, grim-faced.

Jake paused. "You go on ahead," he said to the officers. "I've got one or two things to check here."

"Don't you want to see the bodies, Lieutenant?" O'Grady asked.

Jake shook his head. "I've seen enough dead bodies," he said shortly. He turned to the young woman with the red hair.

"Lieutenant Strogani, ma'am. Can you tell me what happened?"

"Oh, yeah, sure." The young woman managed the thinnest of smiles. "I'm Rebecca Graham, junior partner in Smith, Knight & Winter. Mr Minton invited all the partners here tonight, to celebrate the agreement for our firm to represent Minton Associates in its future dealings."

"Uh, huh," Jake said. "I assume we're talking big bucks here?"

Rebecca nodded. "Minton Associates is the biggest financial planning company in this state and five others, and moving into new areas like property development. We estimated the contract could be worth as much as five million dollars."

"The partners must have been pleased to get a contract that size."

"Well, yeah. And a bit surprised, too. I mean, I suppose you know that before they set up in practice, the senior partners here worked in the state prosecutor's office. They were the people who got Mr Minton sent down all those years ago. I guess it just goes to show that he doesn't bear a grudge."

That would explain why the names of the partners seemed familiar, Jake thought. "So what happened when you arrived?" he asked.

"The junior partners got here first. That's expected, of course. Mr Minton welcomed us in, and insisted we have a glass of his home-made punch." Rebecca made a sour face. "I don't know what was in it, but it was icy cold and tasted strong. We each had one glass - actually we downed them pretty quickly - then he took us to the lounge, where the caterers had set up the buffet. We chatted to Mr Minton, ate, drank his vintage wines and admired his paintings - all the things you do at a party."

"And Mr Minton was with you the whole time?"

"Oh yes. I was talking to him."

Jake scratched his head. "So when did the senior partners arrive?"

"An hour or so later. First of all Mr and Mrs Smith, then Mrs Winter, then Mr Knight."

"And Mr Minton was pleased to see them too?"

"Certainly. He made them try the last of his punch, then they came up here and joined in with the party."

"What about the food? Did they have anything special?"

"You mean, did Mr Minton set aside special canapés for the senior partners?" Rebecca gave a short laugh. "Seniority doesn't extend that far, lieutenant. They had sandwiches, dips, vol-au-vents - just like the rest of us."

"And when did you first realise anything was wrong?"

Rebecca bit her lip. "It must have been about half-an-hour after the senior partners got here. Mr Smith just doubled over. At first I thought he'd choked on a sandwich or something. Mrs Smith rushed over, and the next thing I knew both of them fell to the floor. Mrs Winter said she'd call an ambulance, but before she could do anything, she collapsed as well."

"And Mr Knight?"

Rebecca nodded. "He'd gone to the rest room, so we didn't realise at first. By the time the ambulance arrived, all four were dead."

Jake asked Rebecca a few more questions, but there was little more she could add. He thanked her, then continued to the lounge where the bodies were awaiting forensic examination. Someone had covered them with sheets, and that was fine by Jake. He had no wish to confirm how dead they were.

Raph Minton himself was in the lounge, his long face a study in anguish. "Lieutenant Strogani, what a terrible business. I've told your officers everything I know, but if I can be of any further assistance..."

Jake took one look at Raph Minton and knew he was lying. Beyond a doubt, he had murdered all four senior partners. But how had he done it? That was the question a jury would need answered.

In his office, Jake studied his notes again. Minton had a motive, all right - revenge on the team of lawyers who, thirty years ago, had put him away for murder. But what was the method? Somehow, he felt sure, the answer was in the punch; but there had been only enough for one glass per guest; and by the time everyone had been served, the bowl was empty. And anyway - Jake scratched his head - all the guests that night had drunk the punch, and the junior partners had experienced no ill-effects. Neither could Minton have tipped poison into the bowl during the evening. Rebecca was adamant that Minton was with her in the lounge the whole time.

Then, suddenly, the pieces fell into place. Jake hit the side of his head with his fist. Of course! That was how Minton had done it. He picked up the phone. Tomorrow, his own face would be on the front page of every newspaper in town, while Minton's ugly mug would be where it belonged - back behind bars!

Jake had correctly assumed that Minton was guilty of murdering the lawyers who had put him away all those years ago - but, considering all the evidence, how had he managed to poison only them and not his earlier guests?

SOLUTION

The poison was in the ice cubes, which Minton had put into the punch before anyone arrived. As ice melts relatively slowly, those who had drunk the punch early in the evening survived. Those who arrived later, however, drank a deadly potion.